MEMORABLE GREETINGS

I0123423

By

Jeanne "Bean" Murdock

Library of Congress Control Number: 2022906355
ISBN: 9798986094809

Cover image by Jim Tyler, edited by Jeanne "Bean" Murdock

This book is intended for adults only.

TABLE OF CONTENTS

PREFACE

So many greeting cards and so few to choose from . . . that are actually funny. *Memorable Greetings* includes 800 one-liner jokes that you can either add to a standard greeting card or write in a blank card. The joke in your handwriting will seem unique, clever, personalized, and your creation. Take credit for it!

Whether you like edgy jokes, black comedy, political, romantic, seductive, or sarcasm, this book is for you. If you get offended easily, believe in political correctness and censorship, don't know the actual definition of racism, or can be labeled as a "snowflake," then put this book down and run for the hills. *Memorable Greetings* was created for people who aren't afraid to speak their minds and who love a good laugh—at your expense.

If you are one of those people who should be running for the hills, then next time you open a greeting card open it slowly. Your friend may own this book.

INTRODUCTION

At the end of each section you'll see pages with NOTES at the top. These pages allot space for you to keep track of the jokes you used—date and recipient. Example: #11, John W., 2022

I left out the obvious additions to your greetings, for example: Dear _____, Happy St. Patrick's Day. Love, _____. In other words, I focused on the joke. You add the recipient's name and a salutation.

You can write the set up of the joke on the front of the card and write the punchline on the inside.
Example:
Being the black sheep of the family isn't so bad.
It's better than being the blue whale.
The underlined section goes on the front of the card, and the italicized section goes on the inside. Be sure to keep all of the punctuation so as to retain the meaning of the greeting. Don't underline or italicize.
If you are writing your greeting on one page, then just write it all together. For example: Being the black sheep of the family isn't so bad. It's better than being the blue whale.

See the next page for a card sample. I envision *Memorable Greetings* being written on blank cards, which can be purchased by the box—much less expensive than a standard greeting card.

Chapter 1, #10

SECTION I

SPECIAL OCCASIONS

CHAPTER 1

BIRTHDAYS

1. Happy 18th birthday. You no longer have to tell your parents everything,
   and they no longer have to pay for everything.

2. You can have your cake and eat it, too. Let's face it, though.
   You would have been happy with just the frosting.

3. Smile. It's your birthday.
   You made it one more year without dentures.

4. You have been an inspiration to the family.
   Did I say inspiration? I meant perspiration.

5. As you get older, don't worry about memory lapses.
   You won't remember them anyway.

6. Happy Birthday to someone who shares my genes,
   but not my mutations.

7. You're not old, yet.
   You don't have to bounce to get out of a chair.

8. Before you blow out your candles, choose your wish carefully.
   We, too, are hoping you'll win the lottery.

9. Feeling old is relative.
   Getting old is absolute.

10. Being the black sheep of the family isn't so bad.
    It's better than being the blue whale.

11. Happy Birthday to a star on our family tree.
    It's better than being a bad apple.

12. We have the same complexion, the same laugh, the same quirks.
    Fortunately, I don't have your same age.

13. We have the same complexion, the same laugh, the same quirks.
    Fortunately, you don't have my same age.

14. Do you remember the last time the family celebrated a birthday?
    Me either. Thanks for bringing the beer. Cheers!

15. Your birthday is an excuse to get the family together.
    Thanks a lot. Happy Birthday anyway!

16. I may forget other family occasions, but not your birthday.
    Thanks for reminding me.

17. Here is some advice on your birthday. Avoid speed dating. The average participant is 35-65 . . .
    . . . inches around the waist.

18. They say that eating increases your metabolism.
    May your birthday cake make you skinny.

19. I was going to buy you a Happy 29th Birthday card, but the store cut me off.
    "Eleven years is enough!" Happy 40th!

20. I was going to buy you a Happy 39th Birthday card, but the store cut me off.
    "Eleven years is enough!" Happy 50th!

21. Stay healthy so that you can walk well enough
    to look for your glasses and teeth.

22. Your age this birthday is
    an astronomical sign.

23. Not even an astronomer could find a blemish on you.
    You look great!

24. You're not old; you're just mature,
    like a banana you would only use for baking.

25. Are you getting younger?
    Or are you happy to see me?

26. You look great!
    You take the (birthday) cake!

27. Happy Birthday Eve.
    Open a present tonight—just like Christmas.

28. You know you've been single for too long if
    you're cooking your own dinner tonight.

29. I look forward to your birthday—
the time of year when I buy you something I've been wanting.

30. I remember the day you were born
and the broken condom the day you were conceived.

31. You may not have been planned, but
you are definitely loved!

32. Don't hate me for reminding you of your birthday.
I am hoping you'll share the complimentary dessert.

33. Having another birthday is better than the alternative:
your other half being a year older.

34. Your birthday falls on Easter this year.
Let the candy fall where it may.

35. Open this card quickly.
Sorry I didn't have a chance to go to the bank.

36. Open this card slowly.
Here's a little something, but you're worth a million bucks.

37. You're not old, yet.
You don't fart when you do crunches.

38. You're not old, yet.
Your teeth don't fall out when you sneeze.

39. <u>There is a correlation between how old you are and</u>
    how many used tissues are in your clothes.

40. <u>You know you're getting old if</u>
    every morning you have to re-learn how to walk.

41. <u>Your birthday falls on St. Patrick's Day this year—</u>
    and every year. You're lucky!

42. <u>Your birthday falls on Halloween this year—</u>
    and every year. How scary!

43. <u>Your birthday falls on Christmas this year—</u>
    and every year, for Christ's sake.

44. <u>Your birthday falls on New Year's Eve this year—</u>
    and every year. I'll drink to that!

45. <u>I remembered your New Year's birthday.</u>
    I didn't drop the ball!

46. <u>Your birthday falls on Thanksgiving this year—</u>
    Go wild, turkey!

47. <u>Your birthday falls on Valentine's Day this year—</u>
    and every year. That warms my heart!

48. <u>Your birthday falls on the 4th of July this year—</u>
    and every year. No wonder your eyes sparkle.

49. <u>I'm happy to celebrate my man's special day.</u>
    Interesting. You two have the same birthday.

NOTES

NOTES

NOTES

Here are age-specific greetings, ten for each gender. You can start the sentence with something like "Now that you are 20, that age has new meaning . . ." Let's use the first entry below as an example. <u>Now that you are 20, that age has new meaning:</u> *the number of times you heard a professor remind you that you're not in high school anymore.* Or, <u>You are 20!</u> *the number of times you heard . . .* Or, <u>Now that you are 20, you can identify with that age:</u> *the number of times you heard . . .*

20: Men

1. The number of times you heard a professor remind you that you're not in high school anymore.
2. The number of times your parents will ask you when you are going to graduate.
3. The number of times you considered dropping out of college.
4. The number of times you pictured your parents beating you over the head.
5. The number of careers you considered.
6. The number of times you practice your best pick-up line before use.
7. The number of times you will say, "It's not you; it's me."
8. The number of times you will receive a kiss on the forehead at the end of a date.
9. The number of times you will consider kissing your best girlfriend.
10. The number of seconds you hold your breath just to make your chest look bigger.

NOTES

20: Women

1. The number of times you heard your professor remind you that you're not in high school anymore.
2. The number of times your parents will ask you when you are going to graduate.
3. The number of times you considered dropping out of college.
4. The number of times you pictured your parents beating you over the head.
5. The number of careers you considered.
6. While at a bar, the number of times you put your hair behind your ear, unknowingly, to get a guy's attention.
7. The number of times per day you check your messages to see if He called.
8. The number of times per day you say, "He's history."
9. The number of girls you have in your posse.
10. The number of outfits you try on before a date.

NOTES

16

30: Men

1. The number of pounds you've gained since college.
2. The number of times you will hear that this decade will be the best years of your life.
3. The number of opinions you will seek before buying your first home.
4. The number of times your parents asked you when you are getting married.
5. The number of times your parents asked you when they will have grandchildren.
6. The number of days per month you will recite, "I'm sorry. It's my fault."
7. The number of times you re-drafted your résumé.
8. The amount of acreage you want after living in an apartment.
9. The number of colognes you tried.
10. The length, in feet, of your dream boat.

NOTES

18

30: Women

1. The number of pounds you've gained since college.
2. The number of times you will hear that this decade will be the best years of your life.
3. The number of opinions you will seek before buying your first home.
4. The number of times your parents asked you when you are getting married.
5. The number of times your parents asked you when they will have grandchildren.
6. The number of self-help books on your shelves.
7. The number of online dates you scheduled.
8. The number of online dates that were no-shows.
9. The pairs of shoes you have and no longer wear.
10. The number of bikini wax appointments you scheduled and cancelled.

NOTES

40: Men

1. Favorite musical group: UB40.
2. The number of times you reminded your parents of your age, because they can't believe that they have a child that old.
3. It's the new 30. Whatever.
4. How many meters you can walk before getting tired.
5. How many pounds you'd gain if you ate as much as you did when you were 20.
6. How often you question the price of a haircut, since you have less hair.
7. How fast you go in a 25 mph zone, so that your friends don't notice you're driving a minivan.
8. The number of times you told your wife that the garage is off limits.
9. "40 bottles of beer on the wall . . ." is how you start a popular song, because you no longer tolerate more alcohol than that.
10. Your waist circumference.

NOTES

40: Women

1. Favorite musical group: UB40.
2. The number of times you reminded your parents of your age, because they can't believe that they have a child that old.
3. It's the new 30. Whatever.
4. How many meters you can walk before getting tired.
5. How many pounds you'd gain if you ate as much as you did as when you were 20.
6. The number of lines you count on our face.
7. The number of times per day you count the lines on your face to make sure that it's not more than the last time you counted.
8. How many outfits you still have from the '80s.
9. The number of times you changed your lipstick shade.
10. The number of times you hid the remote from your husband.

NOTES

50: Men

1. The number of minutes it takes to get ready to leave the house—just to find your keys.
2. The number of times you heard your doctor say, "It's just stress."
3. The level of decibels you can no longer hear.
4. The number of times you told yourself that you have not reached your prime, yet.
5. The number of friends you'd like to have who are older than you.
6. The number of AARP correspondences you will throw in the garbage.
7. While watching a home repair show, the number of times you'll say, "I can do that."
8. The number of ways you will comb over your bald spot.
9. The number of weeks you will spend in your mid-life crisis.
10. The number of pounds you *actually* bench press.

NOTES

26

50: Women

1. The number of minutes it takes to get ready to leave the house—just to find your keys.
2. The number of times you heard your doctor say, "It's just stress."
3. The level of decibels you can no longer hear.
4. The number of times you told yourself that you have not reached your prime, yet.
5. The number of friends you'd like to have who are older than you.
6. How many times you considered wearing a two-piece bathing suit next summer.
7. How many times you laughed at the thought of wearing a two-piece bathing suit next summer.
8. How many miles you will drive for a low-fat dessert.
9. The number of hot flashes you will have in a 24-hour span.
10. The number of trips you half-planned.

NOTES

60: Men

1. It's the new 50. Whatever.
2. The number of times you will pass yourself off as 65 for the senior discount.
3. The number of inches you hold paper away from your eyes so that you can read it.
4. The number of excuses you will use before finally starting an exercise program.
5. The age that you will consider young when you're 80.
6. The amount of money you pay neighbor kids to do yardwork that you can no longer do.
7. The number of times per year your wife nags you to get a physical.
8. The number of times you will say, "When I was your age . . ."
9. The number of golf courses you will play.
10. The number of ties you will discard.

NOTES

30

60: Women

1. It's the new 50. Whatever.
2. The number of times you will pass yourself off as 65 for the senior discount.
3. The number of inches you hold paper away from your eyes so that you can read it.
4. The number of excuses you will use before finally starting an exercise program.
5. The age that you will consider young, when you're 80.
6. The amount of items you will order on QVC.
7. The number of hair dyes you tried.
8. The number of anti-aging products you tried.
9. The number of times that you will hear that you are the matriarch of the family, in other words, the old female.
10. The number of holiday meals you prepared.

NOTES

32

70: Men

1. The number of times you will be disappointed that you weren't carded for the senior discount.
2. The number of seconds you need to hold each stretch that helps you get out of bed in the morning.
3. The number of times you cancelled an appointment to get hearing aids.
4. The number of times you asked, "What?" in the last hour.
5. The number of RV campgrounds you will visit.
6. The number of grey hairs you counted—before you went bald.
7. The number of times you considered going back to work—just for some alone time.
8. The number of sheep you count to fall asleep at night.
9. The number of times you used your age as an excuse for not exercising.
10. The number of minutes you spend per day hand-watering your prize lawn.

NOTES

34

70: Women

1. The number of times you will be disappointed that you weren't carded for the senior discount.
2. The number of seconds you need to hold each stretch that helps you get out of bed in the morning.
3. The number of times you cancelled an appointment to get hearing aids.
4. The number of times you asked, "What?" in the last hour.
5. The number of RV campgrounds you will visit.
6. The number of driving test appointments you will schedule and cancel.
7. The number of times you will ask, "When will I get to see my grandkids?"
8. The number of volunteer jobs you will have.
9. The number of women's groups you joined.
10. The number of cookbooks you own.

NOTES

80: Men

1. The number of seconds it took you to realize you were drooling.
2. The number of tennis balls you will go through . . . on your walker.
3. The number of millimeters your skin sagged.
4. The number of times you re-drafted your will.
5. The number of times your children suggested a retirement home.
6. The number of times you told your doctor, "It only hurts when I pee."
7. The number of times you will fake a fall, just to get a cute, young girl to help you up.
8. The number of times you will wish that you had remembered to take Viagra.
9. The number of prescriptions you will fill in a year.
10. The number of times per day you check your pulse, just to make sure you're still alive.

NOTES

38

80: Women

1. The number of seconds it took you to realize you were drooling.
2. The number of tennis balls you will go through . . . on your walker.
3. The number of millimeters your skin sagged.
4. The number of times you re-drafted your will.
5. The number of times your children suggested a retirement home.
6. The number of times you will ask your doctor, "I have a prolapsed what?"
7. The number of half-used tissues in the house.
8. The number of half-used tissues in your clothes.
9. The number of times you tried to pass yourself off as 90, just so that people will say, "Wow! You look great."
10. The number of years for which you are grateful.

NOTES

40

CHAPTER 2

WEDDING/ENGAGEMENT

1. You're not good at statistics, are you?
   May you beat the odds.

2. You always did enjoy gambling.
   May you beat the odds.

3. You should have your reception near DMV, so that you won't have to go far
   to drive each other crazy.

4. I promise not to do the math when you announce
   a baby's on the way.

5. Don't worry about having a "celebrity" wedding.
   It comes with a prenuptial agreement and a nasty divorce.

6. It's OK that your proposal wasn't aired in primetime.
   It's better than having your divorce aired in syndication.

7. Ignore the people who say you robbed the cradle.
   You robbed the delivery room.

8. I knew you had a high tolerance
   for pain.

9. Save money and get rings tattooed on your fingers—
   in pencil.

10. <u>Remember, marriage isn't suitable for</u>
impulse shoppers.

11. <u>Thanks for hiring the stripper.</u>
It was nice not having to pay this time.

12. <u>Marriage is like lactose.</u>
Humans weren't meant to tolerate it, but some people can.

13. <u>Women demand a diamond wedding ring in order to</u>
etch the commitment in glass.

14. <u>Women demand a diamond wedding ring as a promise</u>
to afford a divorce attorney.

15. <u>May your honeymoon be in a land far away—</u>
from in-laws.

16. <u>I didn't get you anything from your gift registry, except a gravy boat</u>
with a refugee.

17. <u>I didn't get you anything from your gift registry.</u>
I'm waiting to re-wrap the reception party favor.

18. <u>I'm attending your wedding and all you get from me</u>
is this lousy card.

19. <u>Sorry I won't be attending your wedding.</u>
I promise to make your funeral.

20. Sorry I won't be attending your wedding.
    Get lei'd for me. It's been a while.

21. I'll be able to attend your wedding if
    the reception party favor is a plane ticket.

22. America's most eligible bachelor is off the market.
    Darn.

23. America's most eligible bachelorette is off the market.
    Darn.

24. Don't return your unwanted gifts.
    I'll take them.

25. I'm so happy you two found each other.
    May you be lost in love.

26. You dreamt of this special day ever since you were a little girl.
    Who was the lucky guy?

27. You two are a match made in heaven.
    May you always see stars when you kiss.

28. You two are a match made in heaven.
    May you be in the clouds during your honeymoon.

29. It's a good sign that your wedding is in the spring.
    May you two blossom and grow together.

30. It's been fun watching your storybook lives.
    Remember to name a chapter after me.

31. Please don't elope.
    I'm hoping to catch the bouquet at the reception.

32. Please don't elope.
    I'm hoping to catch the garter at the reception.

33. Please don't elope.
    I'm hoping to meet a single gal at the reception.

34. Please don't elope.
    I'm hoping to meet a single guy at the reception.

35. May your love soar above the clouds,
    and your souls stay grounded.

36. I wanted to buy you a gift basket, but
    the hot air balloon didn't fit in my car.

37. A beach wedding is a great idea!
    Sand, surf, and sea. In wedded bliss you'll be.

38. A beach wedding is a great idea!
    You always liked Marine life.

39. May all of your gifts be of gold,
    as you two are sure to be married 50 years.

40. Don't consider each other a project.
    Too many of those go unfinished.

41. I promise not to cry during the ceremony.
    I get sad when I see how much better you look in a dress than I do.

42. <u>Ignore the wedding tradition of something old,</u>
    <u>something new . . .</u>
    someone divorced.

43. <u>. . . something borrowed, something blue.</u>
    Cupid's arrow struck you two.

44. <u>Something old, something new.</u>
    The hand you hold is the hand that's true.

45. <u>. . . something borrowed, something blue.</u>
    Which refers to your fiancée?

46. <u>Something old, something new.</u>
    Tell me when the baby's due.

47. <u>. . . something borrowed, something blue.</u>
    Which refers to your fiancé?

48. <u>A beach wedding is a great idea!</u>
    You always liked sailors.

49. <u>A beach wedding is a great idea!</u>
    May your single life be permanently cast away.

50. <u>A beach wedding is a great idea!</u>
    You always had a thing for mermaids.

51. <u>A beach wedding is a great idea!</u>
    Wear sunscreen. You don't want to get burned again.

52. <u>Keep track of your clothing on your honeymoon.</u>
    You don't want to lose your shirt.

NOTES

NOTES

NOTES

CHAPTER 3

BABY SHOWER

1. I want to give you the gift of a child with good behavior,
   but I don't know how to wrap it.

2. I wanted to buy you a diaper Genie,
   but he's booked.

3. You're having another baby!
   I guess the sleepless nights from your last baby made you forget what childbirth was like.

4. Remember when your baby comes, don't wear clothes you care about.
   While teething, your baby will drool worse than a St. Bernard.

5. I guess you measured your husband's head circumference
   AFTER you agreed to have children with him.

6. I want to give you epidural as a gift,
   but my doctor won't write the prescription.

7. Buying whipping cream and cherries
   isn't exactly family planning.

8. I'll pretend that your wedding was
   longer than nine months ago.

9. Don't try too hard to make your child a star.
   The only gig he might land is "Celebrity Rehab."

10. I was relieved to hear you are pregnant.
    I almost bought you a gym membership.

11. Forget about Baby Bjorn.
    I'll see about getting you Bjorn Borg.

12. Despite popular belief,
    you don't have to name your baby after the place where he was conceived.

13. I tasted all of the baby food jars
    in hopes of winning that guessing game.

14. Now I know why I heard a
    shotgun at your wedding.

15. I hope that your baby has your eyes, your husband's smile,
    and my wit.

16. Your baby will have your iron, folic acid,
    and sleep.

17. I'm looking forward to the big reveal—
    who the father is.

18. Don't get too hung up on your baby's gender.
    It may change in the next 18 years.

19. I'm sure your child will latch on just fine
    to your money, car keys, and last nerve.

20. The world is about to become a richer place
    with your mini-me on the way.

21. I already know what you will declare during the gender reveal.
    "Straight!"

22. I bombed the SAT, but
    I'm determined to pass the baby food taste test.

23. Your school test scores weren't high, but
    you passed the pregnancy test.

24. Your pregnancy test came back positive
    for a broken condom.

25. Feel no shame in raising your baby alone.
    You got pregnant alone.

26. According to my math, your baby was conceived in November.
    Turkey basters have multiple uses!

27. I wasn't sure what color onesie to buy, so
    I bought one in a mauve.

28. You don't care what gender baby you're carrying, just that the baby is
    wealthy.

29. It's said that babies are close to soul.
    May she sing like Aretha Franklin.

30. It's said that babies are close to soul.
    May he sing like Marvin Gaye.

31. You haven't chosen a baby name, yet.
    Let's make sure you have my correct spelling.

32. It's almost time to start a college fund.
    Great! I want to go back to school.

33. Your baby will have your features
    and an uncanny ability to deliver mail.

34. Your baby will have your features
    and an uncanny ability to deliver milk.

35. I'm honored to be your baby's godmother—
    the best type of mother.
    No childbirth required!

36. I'm honored to be your baby's godmother—
    the best type of mother.
    No stretch marks!

37. Baptize your baby twice—
    once to wash away your sins.

38. You two will christen your baby.
    What did you christen when you conceived the baby?

39. If you circumcise your baby, then he might
   cut you out of his will.

40. Circumcision is a big decision.
   Bigger for some boys than others.

41. Forget about "What to Expect When You're
   Expecting?"
   What will the teen years be like?

42. This isn't your first rodeo,
   and your baby's father isn't your first cowboy.

43. This isn't your first rodeo,
   and your baby's mother isn't your first cowgirl.

44. After your baby is born, will he
   do the walk of shame?

45. After your baby is born, will she
   do the walk of shame?

46. Hopefully when your baby first utters, "Mommy,"
   he will be looking at you.

47. Hopefully when your baby first utters, "Mommy,"
   she will be looking at you.

48. Hopefully when your baby first utters, "Daddy,"
   he will be looking at you.

49. Hopefully when your baby first utters, "Daddy,"
   she will be looking at you.

NOTES

54

NOTES

NOTES

CHAPTER 4

ANNIVERSARY

To couple, gay

1. <u>Men. Can't live with them, shouldn't marry them.</u>
   But, you did.

2. <u>I know you're out of the closet.</u>
   You two don't sit with an empty seat between yourselves in public.

3. <u>I knew you two were an item.</u>
   You wear pink.

4. <u>You're the most handsome couple I've ever met.</u>
   And the most I wish were single.

5. <u>You're the most handsome couple I've ever met.</u>
   And the most I wish were straight.

6. <u>Which one of you forgets</u>
   your anniversary?

7. <u>You made it another year.</u>
   I knew you chose wisely.

8. <u>You two are a power couple!</u>
   Glad you made it another year without a power struggle.

To couple, lesbian

9. <u>Women. Can't live with them, shouldn't marry them.</u>
   But, you did.

10. <u>I knew you two were an item.</u>
    You don't wear pink.

11. <u>You're the most beautiful couple I've ever met.</u>
    And the most I wish were single.

12. <u>You're the most beautiful couple I've ever met.</u>
    And the most I wish were straight.

13. <u>You made it another year.</u>
    I knew you chose wisely.

14. <u>Which one of you remembers</u>
    your anniversary?

15. <u>You two are a power couple!</u>
    *Glad you made it another year without a power
    struggle.*

16. <u>I debated between a traditional and modern gift.</u>
    Traditional suits my home much better!

17. <u>Paper is the traditional gift for first anniversary.</u>
    For the second anniversary traditional is a shredder.

18. <u>Traditional third anniversary gift is leather.</u>
    Oooh! I hope you have a gift registry.

To couple, any

19. You've been married long enough, now, that
    there aren't many people left in the betting pool.

20. Your love for each other inspires me to choose the right
    partner,
    and your fights remind me to stay single.

21. You've made it this far.
    So, you've shared your lives AND your food.

22. You've made it this far.
    So, you've shared your lives AND your money.

23. Your marriage has lasted a long time.
    You should coach politicians on campaign promises.

24. Your marriage has lasted a long time.
    You've made "'em like they used to."

25. Your relationship has been better than a mediocre real
    estate investment.
    There's been appreciation.

26. You made it another year.
    I knew you chose wisely.

27. You two are a power couple!
    *Glad you made it another year without a power
    struggle.*

To each other

28. Can you believe we made it this far?
    Yes? Oh, yeah. Me, too. Of course.

29. I am loved by all of your heart. I am inspired by all of
    your successes. I am stimulated by all of your
    knowledge.
    And I am funded by all of your wallet.

30. I'm not embarrassed that we met online.
    It's better than meeting on bar.

31. We may not have started our relationship in the most
    respectable way,
    but you have to admit the conjugal visits were fun.

32. I'm grateful that our marriage wasn't arranged,
    but I wouldn't have minded a dowry.

33. I love you for who you are and
    whom you made me.

34. We made it another year!
    We chose wisely!

35. We are a power couple!
    Glad there's no power struggle.

36. I'm grateful that our marriage wasn't arranged,
    but now it could use some rearranging.

37. I'm grateful that our marriage wasn't arranged,
    but could you arrange a threesome?

38. I'm grateful that our marriage wasn't arranged,
    but could you arrange to pick up after yourself?

39. You bring out the funny in me,
    and I bring out the credit card for you.

40. Behind every successful relationship there is
    a wealthy therapist.

41. I love you to the
    bank and back.

42. I feel alive when I'm with you.
    Thank you for breathing life into me.

43. You light up a room when you walk in;
    turn off the light when you leave.

44. Take the o out of love and all you have is
    three letters.

45. What I love most about you is that
    you're all mine!

46. We don't need an anniversary for me to remember
    how fortunate I am to spend my life with you.

47. We don't need an anniversary for you
    to buy me a gift.

NOTES

62

NOTES

NOTES

CHAPTER 5

GRADUATION

High School

1. Now you're off to college, where drug dealers, rapists, and slum lords await.
   Don't worry. You'll be fine.

2. Graduation represents passing all of your classes: drama, cheer, shop, language, humanities, analysis, anatomy, chemistry, in other words
   RELATIONSHIPS.

3. You're flying the coop. Careful where you poop on your way out.
   Your parents sacrificed a lot for you.

4. As you start college, don't confuse dating websites with bank websites.
   You could be matched with debt.

5. As you go off to college, beware of the freshman 15—
   how many years it will take to pay off your student loan.

6. I didn't get to chaperone any of your high school dances.
   I promised not to hit on any of your friends!

7. I didn't get to chaperone your prom.
   I could have finally claimed, "I went to prom."

8. I'm so proud of the adult you became.
    And relieved you didn't end up like me.

9. I'm so proud of the adult you became.
    You are a better version of myself.

10. In my day, I had to avoid the college freshman 5:
    the number of guys trying to get in my pants.

11. You didn't give a valedictorian speech,
    but your plea for a new car was a tear-jerker.

12. Curricular, extra-curricular, co-curricular,
    oh, my, you accomplished a lot.

13. Now put your diploma in a beautiful frame.
    Proudly display your achievement.

14. During your high school years I lived through you
    vicariously.
    Now I know what it's like to earn B's and A's.

15. You have my eyes, my smile, my laugh,
    but not my cumulative GPA, fortunately.

16. You scored well on the SAT:
    sass and tales.

17. You are a model student.
    Looks go a long way, don't they?

18. You're the first in our family to finish high school.
    And the last to clean your room. We're still proud!

College

19. <u>Off into the real world you go. It's called the real world,</u>
because you'll be really broke, really lonely, and really overworked.

20. <u>You're a college graduate, so now you know how to think logically.</u>
You'll need logic to rationalize spending more than you earn, working a job you're over-qualified for, and being in a relationship with someone you're too good for.

21. <u>You're the first in the family to earn a college degree.</u>
And the first to have a student loan!

22. <u>Don't worry about living paycheck to paycheck.</u>
It's better than living loan to loan.

23. <u>You should have held out for an honorary degree.</u>
If Bill Cosby could get one, then you're a shoo-in.

24. <u>You have made our family proud</u>
and my wallet empty.

25. <u>It's OK that you changed majors;</u>
it's better than changing genders.

26. <u>I'm so proud of your commitment to learning.</u>
You're wise beyond your years.

27. <u>You have a degree</u>
of pride—flaunt it.

28. <u>The world is your oyster.</u>
    Don't crack your tooth on the pearl.

29. <u>The world is your oyster.</u>
    Stay away from the raw ones.

30. <u>I'm your fake aunt, but</u>
    I'm as proud of you as if we were blood.

31. <u>I'm your "uncle," but</u>
    I'm as proud of you as if we were blood.

32. <u>Your mother didn't want you to fly the coop, but</u>
    she wanted a crafts room.

33. <u>Your father didn't want you to fly the coop, but</u>
    he wanted a man cave.

34. <u>You stayed within budget, earned good grades, and
    called regularly.</u>
    *We are so proud of how you've blossomed into a mature
    adult.*

35. <u>You stayed within budget, earned good grades, and
    called regularly.</u>
    Are you sure you're our child?

36. <u>Wear your cap and gown proudly.</u>
    You never brought your laundry home to wash.

37. <u>Wear your cap and gown proudly.</u>
    *You earned your degree, independence, and the respect
    of us all.*

38. <u>High school degree. Check. College degree. Check.</u>
    Buy us a house. Check.

39. <u>High school degree. Check. College degree. Check.</u>
    Write us a check. Check.

40. <u>Your achievements and drive inspire me to</u>
    start over and follow in your footsteps.

41. <u>You passed a degree worth of exams.</u>
    Now pass the driver's test!

42. <u>Thanks, big sis', for being a good role model.</u>
    I hope that I can make Mom and Dad just as proud.

43. <u>I missed you while you were at college,</u>
    but it's been nice having two bedrooms.

44. <u>I missed you while you were at college,</u>
    but it's been nice having my own bedroom.

45. <u>Thanks, big bro', for being a good role model.</u>
    I hope that I can make Mom and Dad just as proud.

46. <u>Your cap and gown should come in a color of your
    choice.</u>
    Black is so last season.

47. <u>Your cap and gown should be white to represent</u>
    your bright future.

48. <u>You have brains under your cap and</u>
    clothes under your gown—hopefully.

NOTES

NOTES

NOTES

SECTION II

HOLIDAYS

CHAPTER 6

VALENTINE'S DAY

To a friend

1. <u>May Cupid pierce</u>
   your ex's heart and he bleeds out.

2. <u>May Cupid pierce</u>
   your ex's heart and she bleeds out.

3. <u>Ask Cupid to be your Valentine.</u>
   You like 'em short.

4. <u>Ask Cupid to be your Valentine.</u>
   You like 'em young.

5. <u>You're still single. Maybe you should be a matchmaker.</u>
   Those who can't do . . . teach.

6. <u>Can I, too, be your Valentine? It's OK to have more than one.</u>
   You remember that time in college.

7. <u>Romance, love, surprise, and intimacy await you tonight.</u>
   Too bad it will be in the form of ice cream and a movie.

8. <u>My heart goes out to you</u>
   today and every day.

To partner

9. <u>I love you for all that you do for me,</u>
   and you love me for all that I buy you.

10. <u>Noses are red. Violence is blue.</u>
    Maybe we should lay off the alcohol.

11. <u>I'm glad we met on DateAndDump.com.</u>
    Times up!

12. <u>You said that cheating is a deal breaker.</u>
    Is that all?

13. <u>Marry me again.</u>
    I love bachelor parties.

14. <u>Marry me again.</u>
    I love bachelorette parties.

15. <u>I remember the day we met.</u>
    The years since are a little hazy.

16. <u>I have loved you ever since I saw you</u>
    in the line-up.

17. <u>I have loved you ever since I saw you</u>
    in the want ads.

18. <u>I love your smile, which is as wide as</u>
    my love for you.

19. I have loved you ever since
    the conjugal visit.

20. I don't love you in spite of your quirks; I love you
    because of
    the perks.

21. You said you didn't ask me out sooner than you did,
    because I wasn't ready.
    Your sensitivity is one of the many things I love about
    you.

22. Should we tell our friends about our love affair?
    Well, they were at our wedding.

23. Should we tell our parents we're dating?
    The ladder at my bedroom window might be a
    giveaway.

24. Should we tell our parents about our love affair?
    They're already looking down on us.

25. Thanks for letting me have a mistress.
    Someone needs to cook us dinner.

26. Thanks for letting me have a mistress.
    Now you no longer have headaches.

27. You're my soul mate, which means
    I'll still be writing honey-do lists after we die.

28. Ever since we met
    my heart has whispered for you.

29. <u>I wouldn't change you at all.</u>
    You are such a doll!

30. <u>You're the only one who laughs at my jokes</u>
    and the only one who puts up with my folks.

31. <u>You have made me the man I am today,</u>
    gray hairs and all.

32. <u>Valentine's Day is a day that dentists</u>
    dance around their cash registers.

33. <u>Chocolate and hearts and cookies, oh my!</u>
    Cavities and crowns and dentures, oh crap!

34. <u>Should we tell our parents we're dating?</u>
    The rocks on the window sill might be a giveaway.

35. <u>You meet all of my dating criteria.</u>
    Will you meet all of my exes?

36. <u>You meet all of my dating criteria.</u>
    Next is the cooking criteria.

37. <u>Our journey has been quite the adventure.</u>
    Can we stay home now?

38. <u>Our journey continues as our love grows stronger.</u>
    If only our garden would grow.

39. <u>You love my kids as your own.</u>
    You are a step-angel!

40. Valentine's Day is on the same day each year—
February 14.

41. Your birthday falls on Valentine's Day this year—
and every year. That warms my heart!

42. I love you to the
bank and back.

43. I feel alive when I'm with you.
Thank you for breathing life into me.

44. You light up a room when you walk in;
turn off the light when you leave.

45. Take the o out of love and all you have is
three letters.

46. What I love most about you is that
you're all mine!

47. We're a square peg and round hole.
No wonder our kids are oblong.

48. Match a square peg with round hole and
you get a heart.

49. We're a square peg and round hole.
No wonder our kids are cross.

50. I don't wonder how you will fit into my planned life.
I wonder what we will plan for our life.

NOTES

80

NOTES

NOTES

CHAPTER 7

ST. PATRICK'S DAY

1. <u>Let's share a six-pack of Guinness—</u>
   an Irishman's Easter basket.

2. <u>May the luck of the Irish bless you</u>
   with not being pulled over for drinking and driving.

3. <u>Is that a leprechaun in your pocket</u>
   or are you happy to see me?

4. <u>Patrick was a saint,</u>
   because he helped his wife with chores.

5. <u>The last Patrick I dated was no saint.</u>
   His idea of dinner and a movie was popcorn at a drive-in.

6. <u>The last Patrick I dated was a missionary.</u>
   He only helped me if I would convert.

7. <u>May you have luck in your pocket</u>
   and Patrick in your pants.

8. <u>May you have a rainbow in your heart</u>
   and a pot of gold in your hands.

9. <u>It's OK to pretend to be Irish, today.</u>
   And it's OK to pretend to be sober, today.

10. Be careful whom you try and out-drink.
    Alcoholics call St. Patrick's Day: Amateur Day.

11. On St. Patrick's Day, Protestants wear orange and Catholics wear green.
    And drunks wear black and blue.

12. On St. Patrick's Day, Protestants wear orange and Catholics wear green.
    I'll be blue . . . sitting at home.

13. Tonight you'll be out painting the town.
    I'll be home green with envy.

14. It's OK to pretend to be Irish, today.
    And it's OK to pretend not to be hungover tomorrow.

15. A four-leaf clover represents good luck.
    May you have a bounty of weeds in your yard.

16. A four-leaf clover represents good luck,
    and a five-leaf clover represents too many beers.

17. It's OK to pretend to be Irish, today, but remember:
    an Irishman can laugh at himself and encourages others to laugh along.

18. St. Patrick cleared Ireland of snakes.
    If only he could clear New York City of rats.

19. St. Patrick cleared Ireland of snakes.
    If only he could clear bank corporate offices of thieves.

20. St. Patrick cleared Ireland of snakes.
    If only he could clear politics of rats.

21. We're having corned beef and cabbage for dinner tonight!
    Thanks for cooking!

22. Corned beef and cabbage go together like
    an Irishman and beer.

23. Red potatoes, yellow potatoes, brown potatoes.
    Let's carbo-load and marathon-shop tomorrow.

24. Have a pint on me
    and a round on you.

25. I'm so excited for St. Patrick's Day I could do an Irish stepdance
    right into your arms.

26. The Irish stepdance originated from
    St. Patrick dodging snakes.

27. The Irish stepdance originated from
    drunks trying to stay upright.

28. St. Patrick's Day is celebrated on March 17, because
    it takes two months to sober up from New Year's Eve.

29. St. Patrick's Day is celebrated on March 17, because
    it allows nine months to sober up before New Year's Eve.

30. <u>Place a St. Patrick's basket by your fireplace.</u>
    Judging by Santa's rosy face, he observes the holiday.

31. <u>Place a St. Patrick's basket by your fireplace</u>
    with ice.

32. <u>May your bread be as corny as</u>
    an Irishman's jokes.

33. <u>I hope your cornbread won't be as dry as</u>
    an Irishman's jokes.

34. <u>Corned beef and cabbage and cornbread, oh my!</u>
    To be stored 'til next year on my thighs.

35. <u>We're green with envy of</u>
    our own love!

36. <u>If I wake up, tomorrow, next to a green person,</u>
    then I'll know you drank too much beer.

37. <u>Are you wearing green make-up or</u>
    are you partying too hard?

38. <u>Don't worry if you hear bagpipes.</u>
    You're not in the Blue Ridge Mountains.

39. <u>I hear bagpipes!</u>
    St. Patrick is on his way!

40. <u>Is that an avocado mask or</u>
    have you been partying too hard?

41. St. Patrick's Day is on the same day each year—
March 17.

42. Your birthday falls on St. Patrick's Day this year—
and every year. You're lucky!

43. We have a beautiful relationship.
May our friends be green with envy.

44. I miss you. If only I could be
the rim of your stein tonight.

45. Patrick, you are no saint.
Thank goodness!

46. I've always wondered what was under a kilt.
Nothing?!

47. Don't confuse St. Patty's Day with
Asia's Rice Paddy's Day.

48. Don't get your knickers in a knot or
your kilt in a wind storm.

49. I love you forever. And I'm not just
blowing wind up your kilt.

50. Happy Corned Beef Patty's Day.
Watch out for the pepper corns!

51. Corned beef, corn bread, pepper corns.
You're having a GMO hootenanny.

NOTES

NOTES

NOTES

CHAPTER 8

EASTER

1. <u>I was going to buy you an Easter basket,</u>
   but the store was out of Guinness.

2. <u>May the powers-that-be</u>
   place a Playboy bunny in your Easter basket.

3. <u>On Easter a Catholic priest will release a dove as a</u>
   <u>symbol of peace.</u>
   Last year he released a Catholic school boy as a
   symbol of . . . heterosexuality.

4. <u>May your eggs be unfertilized</u>
   and you continue your life without children.

5. <u>Don't be a basket case this Easter.</u>
   I'm sure you'll find a bunny covered in chocolate.

6. <u>My favorite holiday is</u>
   nor'easter.

7. <u>Don't put all your eggs in one basket.</u>
   Save one for breakfast!

8. <u>When you're hiding Easter eggs from your children,</u>
   make a note of where you put them (the eggs, not your
   children).

9. <u>There should be Easter egg hunts for adults.</u>
   I'd rather go on a man hunt.

10. Chocolate and bunnies and eggs, oh my!
    Cavities and crowns and dentures, oh crap!

11. Beware of who fills your Easter basket.
    It may be your dentist.

12. May one of your eggs be fertilized
    and your wish to start a family comes true.

13. It's Easter. Hop to it!
    Only a few times a year you can rationalize bingeing on chocolate.

14. Hang a stocking. Place a trick-or-treat basket at your front door. Put an Easter basket by the fireplace.
    Increase your chances of receiving candy.

15. Don't put all your eggs
    in one basket case.

16. The Easter bunny is just a
    chicken in rabbit's clothing.

17. I'm looking forward to the big reveal—
    the gender of the Easter bunny.

18. Pastels are a sign of spring.
    Cavities are a sign of Easter.

19. Need excitement this Easter?
    May I suggest moving the egg hunt to the bedroom?

20. Need excitement this Easter?
    Whipped cream and cherries fit in a basket.

21. Easter falls on your birthday this year.
    Let the candy fall where it may.

22. Easter is on a Sunday so that you can
    eat candy and ask for forgiveness on the same day.

23. I gave up Lent for Lent.
    Who needs moderation?

24. I gave up Lent for Lent.
    Christ suffered?! He never birthed a baby!

25. I gave up Lent for Lent.
    As a parent, by definition I've given up plenty.

26. Hop on over to my house for Easter.
    And keep hoppin' right into my bed.

27. Leave a carrot out for the Easter Bunny Easter Eve.
    The Easter Bunny won't resist temptation.

28. It's no longer politically correct to call Easter eggs colored.
    They're Christian American.

29. You are as colorful as
    an Easter egg.

30. Remember that vertical stripes are slimming.
    Do your eggs justice.

31. Easter is a day that dentists
    dance around their cash registers.

32. Choose the right bunny costume.
    Easter holiday is rated G.

33. Hide your eggs well.
    You don't want to get pregnant!

34. Make your eggs easy to find.
    You're trying to get pregnant, after all.

35. A bunny laying eggs is like
    a hen having a lucky foot.

36. Don't wish for a rabbit's foot in your basket.
    The Easter bunny won't be able to get around.

37. I was a little confused about Easter.
    I colored rabbit feet.

38. Cooking rabbit stew for Easter is like
    roasting an elf for Christmas.

39. Keep your fireplace clear Easter Eve,
    unless you want rabbit stew for dinner.

40. Hare today.
    (Teeth) gone tomorrow.

41. I hope you have a
    Hare-iffic Easter!

42. <u>I only exercise on Wednesday.</u>
    Ash Wednesday.

43. <u>When the collection basket is passed at church,</u>
    take a chocolate.

44. <u>When the collection basket is passed at church,</u>
    offer your emotional baggage.

45. <u>Pastels aren't slimming, but neither is</u>
    chocolate.

46. <u>Pastels aren't your colors, but neither is</u>
    black on Easter.

47. <u>Pastels are synonymous with Easter, because</u>
    after eating too much candy you'll be pale.

48. <u>Hare today, gone tomorrow.</u>
    Come back! I want more candy!

49. <u>Hare today, gone tomorrow.</u>
    Candy today, love handles tomorrow.

50. <u>Hare today, gone tomorrow.</u>
    Candy today, exercise tomorrow.

51. <u>You don't have to dress as a bunny</u>
    to hop on over.

52. <u>We don't have to dress as bunnies</u>
    for us to have a romp.

NOTES

96

NOTES

NOTES

CHAPTER 9

4TH OF JULY

1. Congratulations on your divorce,
   a.k.a. Independence Day.

2. May you see beautiful lights in the sky, tonight,
   and fireworks in the bedroom.

3. May the 4th of July represent Independence
   from debt, parents, political parties, and church.

4. Since the 4th of July is six months from New Year's
   Day,
   celebrate your Independence from resolutions.

5. The British are leaving!
   The British are leaving!

6. Traveling in Great Britain on the 4th of July is like
   traveling in Japan on December 7.

7. "Welcome to the United States. Now go home,"
   George Washington said.

8. Refugees are more than happy to celebrate
   Independence Day in America.

9. You're sporting red, white, and blue:
   *blood-shot eyes, white nose, and blue lips. What have
   you been up to?!*

10. <u>Hang your American flag proudly.</u>
    It's not in every country that you can talk about
    carrying a concealed gun in a church of your choice.

11. <u>If I see your flag flying upside down,</u>
    then I'll know you need to talk. Hang in there.

12. <u>The Declaration of Independence is so</u>
    last century . . . or three.

13. <u>O say can you see</u>
    it's time to party!

14. <u>O say can you see</u>
    I love you!

15. <u>Three-day weekend, here we come.</u>
    God bless America!

16. <u>God bless America,</u>
    band that I love.

17. <u>God bless America (and its beaches),</u>
    sand that I love.

18. <u>Wear your stripes proudly</u>
    and vertically—more flattering.

19. <u>Identify with our flag:</u>
    50 stars—one for each of the many attributes I love
    about you.

20. I love your BBQ parties.
You make the best food this side of the Atlantic.

21. You're as American as apple pie
and as sweet!

22. You're as American as baseball and apple pie,
and as Mexican as a Canadian.

23. I love you as much as I love our country.
There should be a flag for my loyalty to you.

24. In her early 20s, Betsy Ross sewed the first US flag.
In my early 20s, I sowed my oats.

25. In her early 20s, Betsy Ross sewed the first US flag.
In my early 20s, I sewed my first button.

26. In her early 20s, Betsy Ross sewed the first US flag.
In your early 20s, you sowed your oats.

27. When Vermont became the 14th state admitted to the union,
Betsy Ross said, "Dang it!"

28. In 1791 when Vermont became the 14th state admitted to the union,
Betsy Ross told George Washington, "You should have thought of that 15 years ago!"

29. Roses are red, violets are blue,
white is for purity of my love for you.

30. The British call our 4th of July
    Dependence Day.

31. Ooh. Ah. Ooh. Ah.
    May you say, tonight, as you look up at your bedroom ceiling.

32. Congratulations on becoming a US citizen.
    May you assimilate all that The Constitution represents.

33. You are as patriotic as you are charming.
    Run for president!

34. Don't confuse fireworks on the 4th of July with New Year's.
    One set is lit at dusk and the other at drunk.

35. Our country's leaders used to be patriotic.
    Now they're idiotic.

36. Being a slave to our founding fathers was
    better than being a slave to society.

37. The 4th of July is on the same day each year—
    the 4th of July.

38. Traveling in Great Britain on the 4th of July is like
    observing Columbus Day on an Indian reservation.

39. Traveling in Great Britain on the 4th of July is like
    observing Veteran's Day in Vietnam.

40. Those aren't fireworks in the sky.
    They're politicians' agendas blowing up in their faces.

41. Those aren't fireworks in the sky.
    They're celebrities' opinions blowing up in their faces.

42. Those aren't crackling fireworks.
    They're my joints. I'm feeling my age.

43. Your birthday falls on the 4th of July this year—
    and every year. No wonder your eyes sparkle.

44. I would love you to the moon and back, but
    a firework might hit me in the ass.

45. Red, white, and blue,
    bed, night, and you.

46. Run naked through the streets with sparklers.
    You have your freedom!

47. When you run through the streets with sparklers,
    remember your britches.

48. I know you like to party on July 4,
    but a Molotov cocktail is a bit much.

49. I hope your night ends
    in a bang!

50. You have reason to celebrate freedom:
    you don't acquiesce to fake pandemic mandates.

NOTES

NOTES

NOTES

CHAPTER 10

HALLOWEEN

1. Don't be afraid of the zombies you see today.
   They're just people who played too many video games.

2. Dress as you wish.
   Black faces matter.

3. Here's a simple costume idea.
   Put cash in your bra and title your outfit Endowment.

4. You could dress up as someone who doesn't lead a healthy lifestyle,
   but it would be too tiring.

5. Dressing up as a Catholic priest and nun is so passé.
   You two should dress as a Catholic priest and school boy.

6. The coronavirus pandemic ruined
   the fun of wearing a mask.

7. I was going to dress as the Michelin Man,
   but I don't have a spare tire.

8. Don't get angry if someone smashes your pumpkin.
   You'll be that much closer to having pumpkin pie ready for Thanksgiving.

9. Ghosts, ghouls, and goblins, oh my!
   Chocolate, taffy, and suckers, oh yeah!

10. <u>Hang a stocking. Place a trick-or-treat basket at your front door. Put an Easter basket by the fireplace.</u>
Increase your chances of receiving candy.

11. <u>Plastic surgeons' offices are just</u>
expensive Halloween costume shops.

12. <u>There really is no age cutoff for trick-or-treating;</u>
just ask a snow-plow parent.

13. <u>It's easy to remember the days of eating Halloween candy.</u>
Just look at your hips.

14. <u>Halloween:</u>
the only time it's OK to be ghosted.

15. <u>An adult trick-or-treater is better known as</u>
an uninvited guest for dessert.

16. <u>Halloween is the day you see</u>
costumes portraying adults' true selves.

17. <u>Orange is the new jack—</u>
o'-lantern.

18. <u>Orange is the new sack—</u>
of candy!

19. <u>I was going to dress as Marilyn Monroe to greet trick-or-treaters, but</u>
I couldn't get my barbiturate prescription re-filled.

20. Halloween:
    the only time it's OK to ghost someone.

21. It's easy to remember your birthday.
    I'll be sure to carve-out time for you.

22. FYI:
    I won't be opposed to a boo-ty call tonight.

23. Your Halloween birthday is
    carved into my memory.

24. Let's bar-hop in our costumes.
    I'll show you witch way to go.

25. I look forward to spending time with you,
    unless you made a Hallo promise.

26. Don't be a sucker—
    but you can eat one.

27. Halloween is a day that dentists
    dance around their cash registers.

28. Chocolate and licorice and suckers, oh my!
    Cavities and crowns and dentures, oh crap!

29. My dentist can't see me.
    He's up to his teeth in candy corn.

30. Light your jack-o'-lantern.
    Your sweet tart is on her way.

31. <u>Halloween is on the same day each year—</u>
October 31.

32. <u>My optometrist can't see me.</u>
He's cross-eyed from all the candy his kids brought home.

33. <u>One time. In college.</u>
Many times. On Halloween!

34. <u>Boo!</u>
Snared you! I'm the luckiest woman.

35. <u>Boo!</u>
Snared you! I'm the luckiest man.

36. <u>Did you just see a ghost or</u>
are you dressed as Michael Jackson?

37. <u>Did you just see a ghost or</u>
are you dressed as a geisha?

38. <u>Politicians look like ghosts.</u>
I can see right through them.

39. <u>Visiting a cemetery on Halloween is like</u>
shopping on Black Friday.

40. <u>Don't worry. You can't get diabetes from eating candy.</u>
You can only get fat. Phew!

41. <u>Don't worry. You can't get diabetes from eating candy.</u>
You can only get shamed. Phew!

42. Don't worry. You can't get diabetes from eating candy.
You can only get cavities. Phew!

43. Your birthday falls on Halloween this year—
and every year. How scary!

44. Eating candy is a great way to
seek an available dentist!

45. I eat so much candy on Halloween that in my
mouth the dentist can hear his echo echo echo.

46. Forget about looking for razor blades in candy.
Look for nutritional value!

47. Forget about looking for razor blades in candy.
Look for vitamins!

48. Some people pass out candy on Halloween.
I pass out.

49. Some people pass out candy on Halloween.
I pass out dentist gift certificates.

50. Every time I knock on a door,
someone offers me candy. Do I look that scary?

51. Let me give you a little advice.
Don't wear an avocado mask.

52. I was turned away at a masquerade party.
I was wearing a milk mask.

NOTES

NOTES

NOTES

CHAPTER 11

THANKSGIVING

1. <u>We'll be having the usual for dinner.</u>
   Just what this family needs. Another turkey.

2. <u>For dinner there will be the usual dishes:</u>
   criticism, insult, gossip, and argument.

3. <u>I remember the snide remark your spouse made to you.</u>
   Don't pardon that turkey.

4. <u>My dyslexic friend cooked a rabbit for Thanksgiving.</u>
   In five months she'll eat a chocolate turkey.

5. <u>Gobble gobble is a sound a turkey makes,</u>
   not a suggestion for how fast to eat.

6. <u>If chicken is a poor man's turkey, then</u>
   I would live in Beverly Hills if I were a chicken.

7. <u>Christopher Columbus discovered Thanksgiving.</u>
   At least that's what he told his mother.

8. <u>Thanksgiving falls on the fourth Thursday in November.</u>
   Not to be confused with April Fool's Day falling on the sixth Thursday in May.

9. <u>Eating pumpkin pie without whip cream is like</u>
   watching a movie without popcorn.

10. <u>A cornucopia without corn</u>
    is just ucopia.

11. <u>May your Thanksgiving meal include a cornucopia</u>
    and your dessert include no Calor-ia.

12. <u>Toot your own horn. You're a great cook!</u>
    Just wait until after dinner to toot.

13. <u>May your abundance gratitude</u>
    not include body weight.

14. <u>Count your many blessings.</u>
    Forget your many divorces.

15. <u>Give gratitude to checking items off your bucket list.</u>
    You're steps closer to death!

16. <u>Count your many blessings.</u>
    *You haven't been incredibly lucky; you've been
    incredibly wise.*

17. <u>Don't wear white after Labor Day or</u>
    to a feast.

18. <u>If you haven't decorated in fall colors, yet, then</u>
    you're a season late and a pumpkin short.

19. <u>Thanksgiving colors are easy to spot.</u>
    So is the turkey, never arriving right on the dot.

20. <u>Turkey lives matter!</u>
    May your meal be vegetarian.

21. I'm grateful that you cook,
    and you're grateful I clean.

22. Native Americans call Thanksgiving: Black Thursday.
    Turkeys refer to Thanksgiving as: Blackout.

23. Turkeys refer to Black Friday as:
    Survived Another Year.

24. Let's sail off to an undiscovered land
    or stay home and explore each other.

25. I love you more than
    turkey and all the fixings.

26. I'll be wearing my eating pants at Thanksgiving dinner.
    I'm grateful for spandex and elastic.

27. On Thanksgiving, don't let your eyes be bigger than
    your stomach,
    or your waist be bigger than your pants.

28. It's not too late to
    work off last year's meal.

29. Thanksgiving colors are earth tones to prepare you
    for being 6 feet under after dinner and dessert.

30. Birds of a feather flock together, until November.
    Then it's every man—Tom—for himself.

31. You said you're having turkey for Thanksgiving.
    I thought Christopher Columbus was dead.

32. <u>Cattle refer to Thanksgiving as</u>
Passover.

33. <u>Turkeys refer to Thanksgiving as</u>
The Holocaust.

34. <u>Turkeys refer to Thanksgiving as</u>
Ascension Day.

35. <u>Happy Kwanzaa a.k.a.</u>
Black Friday.

36. <u>Turkey lives matter.</u>
May you have them over for dinner.

37. <u>I would give up pumpkin pie to</u>
have you for dessert.

38. <u>Pumpkin pie without whipped cream is like</u>
sex without . . . whipped cream.

39. <u>I'm grateful for having you in my life. You saved me.</u>
Not the turkey, but you saved me.

40. <u>I'm grateful for having you in my life.</u>
You give me love and all the fixins'.

41. <u>The turkey's timer popped up.</u>
Either the turkey is done or it's happy to see me.

42. <u>Time for bed. Let's roost.</u>
At least that's what we'll tell our kids we're doing.

43. Your birthday falls on Thanksgiving this year—
Go wild, turkey!

44. When Native Americans feasted with the pilgrims,
the natives looked for razor blades in the turkey.

45. The pilgrims didn't land on Plymouth Rock;
they ran aground.

46. The pilgrims were vegetarians who ate turkey;
in other words, they weren't vegetarians.

47. The pilgrims were vegetarians, but
they wanted to meat the Native Americans halfway.

48. Who feels more stuffed after Thanksgiving?
You or the turkey?

49. Look for the big turkey in New York's parade
and his frittered campaign promises trailing.

50. Look for the president in New York's parade
and his handlers preventing him from drifting off.

51. Was that Pinocchio in New York's parade or
a politician?

52. I have a leg up on Thanksgiving dinner—
two legs up.

53. I have a leg up on Thanksgiving dinner—
two legs up after dinner.

NOTES

NOTES

NOTES

CHAPTER 12

CHRISTMAS

1. Ah, Christmas:
   a great time to pretend to be religious.

2. Baby Jesus wasn't in a manger.
   His crib was mangy . . . lost in translation.

3. Ah, Christmas:
   The one day of the year when religion isn't so bad.

4. My Dearest Ebenezer,
   Despite all your anger you make children and adults glow with Christmas joy. Your heart light pierces your steel façade and blinds you from seeing the love you truly hold.

5. You are hosting a party where you will be unveiling your Christmas tree.
   Is that all you will be revealing?

6. All you want for Christmas is
   your two front teeth.

7. This Christmas don't blame Christ
   for your debt, stress, and illness.

8. Choose a different holiday to ask for Double Ds.
   Those won't fit down the chimney.

9. I love Christmas—
   *the time of year when I buy you something I've been
   wanting.*

10. Hang a stocking. Place a trick-or-treat basket at your
    front door. Put an Easter basket by the fireplace.
    Increase your chances of receiving candy.

11. Traditional Christmas colors, green and red, represent
    your inner dialogue:
    Stop. Spend(ing). Stop. Spend(ing).

12. I wreath you a Merry Christmas.
    Excuse my lisp.

13. Deck the halls with
    vows of folly.

14. Let there be peace on Earth
    and around the dinner table.

15. Look for Santa in the sky tonight
    and a candy cane under the covers.

16. It is the night before Christmas.
    Let's pretend I'm your mistress.

17. Beware of zombies, even this time of year.
    They are also known as bargain shoppers.

18. Don't be a grinch. Christmas is fun.
    Shop just a tinch. Before you know it you'll be done.

19. Christmas is a day that dentists
    dance around their cash registers.

20. Chocolate and pie and candy canes, oh my!
    Cavities and crowns and dentures, oh crap!

21. Santa Claus is coming to town.
    So there won't be room for in-laws.

22. Don't smoke like a chimney.
    Santa's on his way!

23. It takes a year for elves to build and wrap toys,
    and a few minutes for children to tear through them.

24. My present to you is enveloped with love.
    I ran out of wrapping paper.

25. Traffic lights have Christmas colors:
    Green for shop and red for debt.

26. Your nose is as red as Santa's.
    You must hang out at the same bar.

27. Rudolph and Santa have the same color nose.
    I didn't know the North Pole had a distillery.

28. Santa's workshop is also known as
    man cave.

29. Even Mrs. Claus is banned from
    her husband's workshop.

30. <u>Christmas is on the same day each year—</u>
December 25.

31. <u>Santa Claus avoids the ghetto.</u>
One year his sleigh was up on blocks.

32. <u>Enjoy the present.</u>
May it enrich your future.

33. <u>Yule log hours and hours of shopping.</u>
Don't burn out!

34. <u>Hang mistletoe over the fireplace.</u>
Mrs. Claus won't suspect another late night at the office.

35. <u>Workmen are going in and out of your house.</u>
You hung mistletoe in your entryway, again?

36. <u>You don't have to dangle mistletoe.</u>
I'll kiss you anyway.

37. <u>Holly is like Washington, DC:</u>
full of pricks.

38. <u>If our child is born on Christmas, then we can name the baby Holly or</u>
Douglas Fir.

39. <u>Since Santa works for free, his name is</u>
St. Nickel-less.

40. <u>Your birthday falls on Christmas this year—</u>
    and every year, for Christ's sake.

41. <u>Holy holly!</u>
    You haven't aged a bit!

42. <u>Holy holly!</u>
    You make the best Christmas dinner!

43. <u>Baby Jesus had neglectful parents.</u>
    He was left alone with total strangers—and a sheep.

44. <u>Jesus had attachment disorder.</u>
    Several nannies doesn't equal a mother.

45. <u>Poinsettia me</u>
    to the bedroom.

46. <u>Is that a poinsettia on your front porch</u>
    or a signal that the coast is clear?

47. <u>Since poinsettias originated in Mexico,</u>
    each plant comes with a drug lord.

48. <u>Since poinsettias originated in Mexico,</u>
    each plant comes with a package of chicle.

49. <u>Since poinsettias are native to Mexico,</u>
    they need hot sauce, not water.

50. <u>When I sat on Santa's lap,</u>
    I knew what he wanted for Christmas.

NOTES

NOTES

NOTES

CHAPTER 13

NEW YEAR'S EVE/DAY

1. Choose a resolution
   that no one will blame you for not keeping.

2. Party like it's 1979—
   like the '80s are around the corner!

3. At midnight New York City will drop a ball.
   In San Francisco they will drop their pants.

4. Make each year better than the last . . .
   your life is in your hands.

5. Be careful whom you try and out-drink.
   Alcoholics call New Year's Eve: Amateur Night.

6. At the stroke of midnight, a groundhog will appear
   to tell you how many days your hangover will last.

7. Light fireworks! Ring bells! Blow horns!
   Your year from hell is over.

8. Light fireworks! Ring bells! Blow horns!
   You accomplished a lot this year.

9. Light fireworks! Ring bells! Blow horns!
   A one-night stand awaits you.

10. Party like it's 1989—
    like the '90s are around the corner!

11. <u>Should old "acquaintance be forgot and never brought to mind?"</u>
Yes if they are exes.

12. <u>I'm excited to share another year of my life with you.</u>
Let's make next year better than the last.

13. <u>Happy Two Years!</u>
Of sobriety.

14. <u>Happy Two Beers!</u>
Oops. Sorry. I started partying without you.

15. <u>I wish I could spend New Year's Eve with you.</u>
Someone needs to hold my hair back at the end of the night.

16. <u>I'm looking forward to dancing with you tonight.</u>
Dips, spins, lifts, lunges. Throw me into the new year.

17. <u>A toast to us. May we live happily ever after</u>
or at least until the champagne runs out.

18. <u>A toast to us. May we live happily ever after</u>
or at least until your wife finds out about us.

19. <u>A toast to us. May we live happily ever after</u>
or at least until your husband finds out about us.

20. <u>A toast to us. May we live happily ever after</u>
or at least until your mistress finds out we're still together.

21. At midnight, New York City will drop a ball.
So will a politician.

22. At midnight, New York City will drop a ball.
I will drop my values.

23. Should old resolutions "be forgot and never brought to mind?"
Absolutely!

24. My New Year's resolution is to start exercising
next year.

25. Up, up, and away!
May our values go astray.

26. Toot your horn tonight.
You kicked butt this year.

27. Light up the sky with fireworks and dreams.
You achieve everything you set your mind to.

28. Light sparklers and run down the street naked.
Celebrate the new year and your newfound freedom.

29. May there be beautiful lights in the sky, tonight,
and fireworks in the bedroom.

30. My New Year's resolution is to
become a gay man.

31. My idea of a polar bear plunge is
a big white guy diving into my bed.

32. <u>New Year's Eve is on the same day each year—</u>
December 31.

33. <u>At the stroke of midnight, a groundhog will appear</u>
to tell you how many days you will use your new gym
membership.

34. <u>My idea of a polar bear plunge is</u>
diving into a white hot tub.

35. <u>I look forward to our kiss at midnight</u>
and a baby nine months later.

36. <u>I look forward to our kiss at midnight,</u>
but not the walk of shame.

37. <u>I'm so happy you stumbled into my life.</u>
In a few hours we'll stumble home.

38. <u>A kiss at midnight will seal the deal.</u>
Our bond is steel and love is real.

39. <u>Those aren't fireworks in the sky.</u>
They're politicians' agendas blowing up in their faces.

40. <u>Those aren't fireworks in the sky.</u>
They're celebrities' opinions blowing up in their faces.

41. <u>Those aren't crackling fireworks.</u>
They're my joints. I'm feeling my age. Here's to another
year older.

42. Your birthday falls on New Year's Eve this year—
and every year. I'll drink to that!

43. I remembered your New Year's birthday.
I didn't drop the ball!

44. I know you like to party on New Year's Eve,
but a Molotov cocktail is a bit much.

45. New Year's Eve is too close to Christmas.
We need more than one week to sober-up.

46. I keep every resolution I make,
said no one ever.

47. I'm happy to walk into the next year
holding your hand.

48. You invite me to a New Year's Eve party, and
all you receive is this lousy card.

49. I had fun with you last night.
That was you, right?

50. Last night was a blur. Did we
ever leave the house?

51. Last night was a blur.
I'll just assume we need to go to church today.

52. Pace yourself tonight,
Mario Andretti.

NOTES

NOTES

NOTES

ABOUT THE AUTHOR

Entrepreneur and satirist Jeanne "Bean" Murdock brings a new approach to comedy, fusing observational humor with health and fitness knowledge. Performing on roller skates where she can, her improvised physical comedy is one that has never been done before. Jeanne's sassy, naive perspective wins audience attention, demanding that the show must go on.

As much as Jeanne loves to perform, she prefers writing. She is prolific, penning screenplays, books, and of course her own jokes, to name a few.

Originally from Cupertino, California, Jeanne was given the nickname **Bean** in third grade by her next-door neighbor simply because it rhymed with Jeanne. She studied physical education at Cal Poly and then started **BEAN**FIT Health and Fitness Services in 1992. Three years later, Jeanne was diagnosed with celiac disease, a condition that she included in her teachings. For 22 years she was a health and fitness professional who happened to be a comedian. Now, she is a comedian who happens to be a health and fitness expert.

Qualifications:
California Polytechnic State University, San Luis Obispo
<u>Bachelor of Science in Physical Education</u>
   concentration: commercial/corporate fitness
Graduation Date: June 1991

San Diego State University, San Diego, CA
<u>Nutrition Didactic Program</u>
Verified: May 2002

IMAGE BY JIM TYLER, EDITED BY GREG HELLER

Questions? Comments? Please feel free to contact
Jeanne "Bean" Murdock anytime.

PO Box 372
Cornville, AZ 86325
Phone: 408-203-7643
Website: www.JeanneMurdock.com
E-mail: laugh@JeanneMurdock.com

Other books by Jeanne "Bean" Murdock
BEANFIT Publishing:

The Every Excuse in the Book Book: How to Benefit from Exercising, by Overcoming Your Excuses

Successful Dating at Last! A Workbook for Understanding Each Other

It's Hard to Find Good Help These Days: A Customer Service Manual for Businesses

That's a Bunch of Quackery! How to Avoid Being Pick-pocketed by Misleading Claims in the Fitness Industry

Serial Good Samaritan

Co-author of Carole Breton's autobiography
My Guardian Angel Wears Antiperspirant
(Stinky Ghost Cat Books 2018)

Not-so ghost writer of Ted Gilbert's autobiography
Barefoot NOMAD
(POGA Publishing 2019)